Peter
the Prince of Apostles

MURIEL F. BLACKWELL • ILLUSTRATED BY PAUL KARCH

BROADMAN PRESS
Nashville, Tennessee

© Copyright 1976 • Broadman Press
All rights reserved
4242-27
ISBN: 0-8054-4427-8

Dewey Decimal Classification: J 225.92
Subject heading: PETER, APOSTLE
Printed in the United States of America

Contents

Boy with a Dream

Simon Hears Some Good News

A Long Night of Fishing

A Promise Made

A Promise Broken

Peter's Second Chance

Sharing the Good News

A Sword and a Prison

Reflections

Boy with a Dream

Young Simon stood on the shore watching the fishermen. Some of the men stood in water which was above their waists; others stood on the sandy shore. Again and again they threw their nets into the water. Simon saw how careful a fisherman was to arrange the round net on his arm before throwing it.

"Ah, Simon, I see you are dreaming again."

Simon turned to see his brother Andrew standing near him.

"But your dreams must be cut short if we get to the synagogue in time for our lessons," Andrew reminded Simon.

"I know," Simon answered Andrew. "But watch, Andrew. See how the big man puts his net exactly where he wants it! And the net does not tangle on his arm as it does for the other fisherman."

Andrew watched as the fisherman cast the net. It fell in the shape of a ring. The weights dragged the net downward. The boys watched as the fisherman pulled on the rope to close the net to trap any fish within.

Simon watched each movement of the fisherman. Then he spoke. "When I grow up, I'm going to be the best fisherman in Bethsaida . . . or maybe even Capernaum. The men say Capernaum is the best spot for

fishing and for selling fish too. I'll probably go to Capernaum. But first I want to learn everything I can about fishing. I want to be the best fisherman ever, Andrew. Don't you?"

   Andrew laughed at Simon's excitement. "Oh, I don't know, Simon, There is plenty of time for work. Right now I'd rather run footraces along the shore with my friends. And I'd like to pick up the pretty shells along the shore."

   Simon turned and put a hand on his brother's shoulder. "That's play, Andrew. But we must also think of ways to earn a living. It's not too early to think of that, now is it?"

Andrew smiled as he turned away from the water. "And I am thinking, Simon, that we better hurry to the synagogue. It is time for lessons, and the rabbi will not be pleased if we are late."

"Oh, lessons," Simon grumbled. "I had hoped to see the big fisherman catch one more netful. Someday I will be able to spend

the whole day with my nets and my own boat. I will catch lots of fish, and people far and wide will know me well."

The two boys walked toward the synagogue. Andrew called to his friends as they walked along. But Simon was in deep thought. He was thinking about the future and his plans for becoming a great fisherman.

Thinkback: Let's call the pages you have just read a "could-have-happened story." Our Bible does not tell us this story, but it does give us clues to point out that these things could have happened. Think about these clues:
1. Simon was a fisherman.
2. Jesus gave him a new name. He was called Peter and sometimes, Simon Peter.
3. He had a brother named Andrew.

4. As a Jewish boy, he probably attended a synagogue school.
5. His early home was Bethsaida where he lived as a boy.
6. When Simon was older, he lived and conducted his fishing business in Capernaum.

• The stories recorded in the Bible about Simon Peter are stories about his life as a grown-up. But you and I know that Peter was once a child like you. He played games with friends. He learned the alphabet (Hebrew) in synagogue school. He learned Scriptures from what we now know as the Old Testament. Quite likely he learned exciting stories from Hebrew history.

• Don't you like to think about Simon Peter as a boy? Just think! He had dreams about growing up just as you do. In the rest of this book, you will read about Simon Peter as a grown-up. But hasn't it been fun to think of him as he might have been as a boy?

Simon Hears Some Good News

Simon was busy cleaning the fishing boat. The nets were drying in the sun. "I wonder where Andrew is," Simon thought. "I have not seen him in a while. It will soon be time to mend the nets for tonight's fishing. I hope he will hurry."

Simon continued to work on the boat as he thought about Andrew. His mind went back to earlier years. He remembered his boyhood days in Bethsaida when he dreamed of becoming a fisherman. He smiled as he recalled that Andrew had never been too excited about the fishing business. Simon recalled his boyish boasts to Andrew. *I want to be the best fisherman ever! Don't you, Andrew? I will catch many fish, and people far and wide will know me well.* Just then, Simon's thoughts were interrupted.

"Simon, Simon!" an excited voice called. Simon looked up to see Andrew coming toward the boat. Simon stepped into the shallow water and waded to the shore. He smiled as Andrew reached him. "Ah, my brother, it is about time you got here. The nets are about dry. We need your quick fingers to help mend them."

"Simon, we cannot mend the nets just now. You must come with me. I have found Jesus, the Messiah!" Andrew's eyes sparkled with excitement.

"Andrew, for many years our people have looked for the Messiah. Others have thought they have found the Christ," Simon said.

Andrew looked at Simon and then out over the blue water of the Sea of Galilee. "I know, Simon. But I have been with the Christ for several hours. I was with John the Baptist, and he called Jesus the Lamb of God! Two of us asked this Jesus where he lived. He then invited us to his house, and we spent the day with him. He is truly the Messiah! I am sure of it. Come with me, and I will take you to him."

So Simon followed the excited Andrew. Soon they reached the spot where Jesus was. Simon stood back a few steps.

"You are Simon, the son of Jona," Jesus said. "I would like to call you Cephas."

Simon was surprised to hear his name called. He was even more surprised to hear the new name this man Jesus had just given him. Simon looked at Jesus. "Cephas," Simon

thought. "That name means a stone. I wonder why I am getting this new name?"

Jesus looked at the two brothers. "Simon, someday men will call you Peter, the Rock." Simon continued to stand quietly in the bright sunshine. He could smell the breeze from the Sea of Galilee. Andrew stood nearby with a smile on his face. He watched Simon as the big fisherman looked at Jesus with a puzzled look at his face.

As they turned away, Andrew spoke: "See, Simon, I told you. Now, are you convinced? Come. Let us finish today's fishing chores. Tomorrow Jesus plans to travel to Galilee. We will go with him to learn more about this Christ that John the Baptist has preached about."

As the brothers walked back to their boat, they spoke little. Simon's mind was filled with many thoughts. *Simon? Cephas? Peter? A Rock? What could all of this mean?* Was this Jesus of whom John preached the long-awaited Messiah? Hadn't the prophets said that he would be called Jesus? And, for the first time in his fishing career, Simon looked at his boat and nets with little interest. His mind was on more important things.

Thinkback: Why was Simon surprised when Jesus spoke to him?

• Which sentences help you to know that Simon was interested in knowing more about Jesus?

A Long Night of Fishing

Peter was unhappy. "What has happened to all the fish?" he said to his fishing partners. "I've thrown my net until my arms hurt. Not one fish have I caught." Peter had never seen such poor fishing on the Sea of Galilee.

"Let's cross over the sea to the other side and try there," James and John suggested. So Peter and his brother Andrew raised the sail on their boat. Then James and John raised the sail on their boat. Soon they reached the other side of the lake. But the fishing was no better there. Over and over they threw the heavy nets into the water. Again and again they pulled in empty nets.

The fishermen fished all night. Finally the sky began to show pink in the east. "Look," Andrew said, "it is almost daybreak. We surely won't catch any fish now."

"No, we might as well go on home," Peter agreed. "I'm so tired, and now we will have to wash these nets."

"And don't forget those holes," Andrew said. "We'll have to mend those."

They called to James and John. Soon the boats were sailing across the Sea of Galilee toward Capernaum.

Peter and Andrew began washing their nets after anchoring their boat. John and James were not far away working on their nets also.

"Look," said Andrew, "I see Jesus coming.

Look at that crowd of people following him! He teaches many hours and still the people follow."

"I know," answered Peter. "It is hard to believe how the people follow him. Since the day you came and told me that you had found the Messiah, I have seen the people who follow him increase in number. He preaches and teaches almost without rest."

The people crowded closer and closer to hear Jesus. Finally they came near the water's edge. Then Jesus stepped into the boat to continue his teaching. Soon he called Peter over and asked him to row the boat out a little ways.

Jesus continued his teaching from the boat. When he had finished talking to the people, he spoke to Peter. "Now row your boat out a little further where the water is deeper. When you get to where the water is deep, let your net down again."

Peter looked at Jesus. "But, Jesus, we have fished all night long and did not catch a single fish," Peter complained. Peter looked at Andrew. His brother was getting ready to do as Jesus said. Peter began to help also. They rowed out to deeper water and dropped the net just as Jesus told them to. Suddenly Peter felt the net grow heavy. There was no mistaking the tug of many fish. He began to

try and pull the net in. Peter's excitement grew. He realized that he and Andrew could not pull the net in by themselves.

"James and John, come quickly!" Peter called excitedly. The fishing partners rowed out to help Peter and Andrew. Soon there were so many fish that both boats were about to sink.

Peter looked around him. He saw the great catch of fish. He remembered the long night just passed without a single fish caught. He remembered his tired, aching arms and his disappointment when dawn came.

Then Peter turned and looked at Jesus. Peter must have thought: *"Who is this man that preaches and teaches long hours? Who is this one that can fill my net with fish?"* Then Peter did an unusual thing. He fell down at Jesus' feet and spoke. "O Lord," I shouldn't be here with you. I am just an ordinary man, a fisherman. Go away from me, O Lord, for I do so many wrong things."

"Listen, Peter," Jesus answered. "You should not be afraid. Just come with me. From now on you will go fishing for men. You will be my helper every day. You will help me preach and teach."

Peter listened quietly. Then he rowed the boat toward the shore. Andrew helped him. James and John rowed their boat toward the shore also. When they reached the shore, Peter jumped from the boat. He forgot about the flopping fish. He forgot about the nets which now needed mending again. He forgot about the boat and his fishing business. Peter looked at Jesus.

"He must be the Messiah, just as Andrew said," thought Peter. For Peter had begun to think about a new kind of fishing. From now on he would follow Jesus. He would learn as Jesus taught and preached. He would help Jesus.

Peter turned and looked quietly at the boat. He saw the sun shining on the fish in the boat. He saw the heavy nets he had pulled in many times. He looked at the people by the seashore as they watched what was happening. Then Peter turned and hurried after Jesus. Andrew, too, followed after Jesus. James and John stepped from their boat. Then they ran along the sandy shore to catch up with Peter, Andrew, and Jesus.

Thinkback: Can you recall two things from the pages you have just read which show that Peter was probably a good fisherman?

- The story of this fishing trip is found in Luke 5:1-11. Which words do you think are the most important ones in this story?

A Promise Made

Peter and John walked along the narrow streets of Jerusalem. The city was crowded. People pushed and shoved in their hurry.

"I am glad we have a room for the Passover supper," Peter said. "The city is so noisy and crowded. It is a good thing Jesus knew how to find the room." John nodded in agreement as the two disciples continued to push their way through the crowds.

Almost three years had passed since that

day when Peter had become an apostle of Jesus. These had been exciting years. Peter had followed Jesus throughout the countryside. He had learned many things as he watched and listened. He had watched as Jesus taught the people, healed the sick, and preached God's message. Peter himself had helped people. He had been sent out by Jesus to teach and preach.

However, things were not going well. Peter was worried. True enough, the people followed after Jesus in great numbers, but the religious leaders were angry with him. They kept trying to trap Jesus in his words. They even stirred up some crowds against Jesus and his apostles. "And to make matters even worse," Peter thought, "Jesus talks in riddles I do not understand. Why just recently he said he would not be with us much longer." Peter shook his head sadly. This week indeed had been a troubled one.

Jesus and his disciples were almost finished with the Passover supper. Peter watched the group. Many things had happened since they had entered the room. The disciples were anxious. Some had even argued about which one of them was the most important. Jesus

had again done things which Peter could not understand. The Master had washed Peter's feet. Then that conversation between Jesus and Judas! And now Judas was gone, swallowed up in the strange, black night. Peter turned his eyes back to Jesus. The Master was speaking.

"I won't be with you much longer. You will wonder where I have gone. For a while you will not understand, but then you will know and understand. I leave an important rule for

you. Love one another the way I have loved you. This way, the people will know that you are my disciples."

Peter sat up, his full attention now on Jesus.

"Lord, where are you going? Peter asked in a puzzled voice. The room was quiet. All ears strained as Jesus answered.

"Where I go, you cannot follow now. Later you shall come."

Peter's eyes sparkled as he spoke directly to the one whom he had followed for three years

now. "Why do you say that I cannot come now? You know I have followed you faithfully. I am ready to do anything for you — even go to prison. And if you have to die as you have been telling us, then I will die with you." All was still in the room. The other disciples listened as the conversation continued.

Jesus looked sadly at Peter. How Jesus loved the big man who spoke so quickly! But Jesus knew what was ahead. "Will you, Peter? Will you die with me? No, Peter. Before the cock crows, you will have said not once, but three times, that you don't even know me."

Peter looked at Jesus. Disbelief showed on Peter's face.

"No, Master. Not even if they kill me. I will never say I do not know you."

Jesus looked away sadly, for Peter was so sure. So very sure.

Thinkback: Find two sentences which help you know that Peter was worried.

- What important rule did Jesus leave for his disciples?
- Is this rule still important for us today? Why?
- What does the word *promise* mean to you? What promise did Peter make to Jesus?

A Promise Broken

Peter shivered in the cold night air. He saw the flickering torches in the distance. His sword tapped against his leg as he stumbled along the dark path. He put his hand on the hilt of the sword. The cold metal sent a

shudder through Peter. How freely he had drawn that sword and used it recently! With one quick stroke he had severed the ear of the enemy. And, equally as quick Jesus had healed the wounded enemy and scolded Peter.

While all eyes were on Jesus, Peter and the other disciples had fled into the shadows of Gethsemane. Where the other disciples had gone, Peter did not know. He only knew that he was alone, and he did not know what to do.

In the distance Peter saw a fire in the courtyard near Caiaphas' house. Soon he was warming himself by the fire. On a porch nearby, Jesus stood among his accusers, his hands tied. Peter looked into the fire and stretched forth his hands to warm them. Suddenly he was aware that a woman was staring at him.

"Here's one of Jesus' followers," she said, pointing a finger. "He was with them."

"You're mistaken, woman. I don't know him," Peter answered. He drew his cloak about him and glanced around. A shadow fell across Peter as another voice spoke.

"You are also one of them. You are a Galilean."

Peter looked at his second accuser. "Man, I swear I don't even know Jesus."

Then another man in the crowd looked closely at Peter "He *is* one of them," the man said loudly. "He is one of the ones I saw in the garden with Jesus tonight."

Then Peter cursed and answered the man.

"I don't even know what you're talking about," he said, turning his back. As Peter's words died away, he heard the unmistakable crowing of a cock. Jesus turned and his eyes met Peter's. No words were spoken. Then Peter forgot his accusers. Silently he counted. One, two, three. Three times he had said he did not know Jesus. Peter's eyes dropped. He could not look at his Master. A lump filled Peter's throat. Tears filled his eyes and spilled down his cheeks. He turned sadly away and walked off into the darkness. By the time he reached the courtyard door he was sobbing. Over and over he reminded himself: *I broke my promise. I broke my promise. I broke my promise.*

Thinkback: In the pages you have just read, some clues are given to show that Peter was afraid. Can you find those clues?

- Have you ever broken a promise to someone you loved. How did you feel? How do you think Peter felt when Jesus looked at him?
- Why is it important to keep a promise?

Peter's Second Chance

Peter and his friends were sitting by Lake Galilee. They were sad. They did not understand all of the things which had happened in the last two weeks. Jesus had been put to death on a cross. This they could recall very well. They also knew that he was alive again because they had seen him. But Jesus was not with them all the time as he had been before his death and resurrection. He was not there to teach them and help them understand God's love. They missed their friend Jesus.

Peter looked out over the water. He remembered with sadness how he had denied Jesus that night in the courtyard. Then he remembered with thankfulness that Jesus still loved him.

After Jesus had risen from the dead, word had been brought from the tomb by the women. A heavenly messenger said: "Tell his disciples *and Peter* that Jesus has gone on to Galilee. They can see him there." Peter's name had been called by itself. To him this seemed to be a personal message, helping Peter know that Jesus had forgiven him. If only he could see Jesus again to tell him that he loved him and would be a faithful disciple!

Peter stood up and brushed sand from his robe. "I am going fishing," he said to his friends.

"We'll go with you," the others said.

Early the next morning, Peter and his friends saw someone standing on the shore. He called to them. "Have you anything to eat?" More conversation followed. Finally John turned to Peter and spoke.

"It is the Lord!"

Peter's heart pounded within him. He tied his fisher's coat around him, jumped into the sea, and swam ashore. The other disciples hurried also. When they reached the shore, they found Jesus preparing food for them. "Come and eat," he said. How glad the disciples were to share another meal with their beloved teacher!

When they had finished eating, Jesus turned to Peter. "Peter, do you love me?"

"Of course, Jesus. You know I love you."

Three times Jesus asked Peter this question. Three times Peter answered yes. And each time Peter felt a little sad that Jesus had asked again. The last time the question came, Peter said:

"Lord, you know everything. Surely you can tell that I do love you."

"Then you are to help guide my followers," Jesus said.

"A second chance!" Peter thought, for Jesus had just given him a job to do.

Thinkback: Can you find the clue which Peter felt helped him know that Jesus had forgiven him?

- When Peter said he loved Jesus, Jesus gave him a special assignment. Read this assignment in John 21:15-17. Find the words in this story which mean the same thing.

Sharing the Good News

Peter looked around the room. He missed Jesus who had gone back to heaven. Yet, how good it was to see the followers of Jesus praising God! "Things are happening just as Jesus said they would," Peter thought. "He said he would send his Holy Spirit to guide us. Now we will know what to do! Now I will know how to lead those who want to obey Jesus' teachings."

Soon the followers of Jesus went out from the room to witness. Peter stood to preach. He spoke boldly. He was not afraid anymore, for Jesus had promised to be with him. Peter told the people that Jesus was alive forever. He reminded the people how they had seen Jesus preach, teach, and heal the sick. "Then you helped to crucify him," Peter went on. "But this same Jesus, God raised from the dead. He is both Lord and Christ."

The people who were listening no longer made fun of the followers of Jesus. Something was happening to the listeners. They did not like to remember the things they had done to

Jesus. They did not wish to be reminded of their sins.

"What must we do?" they asked.

"Repent and be baptized," Peter answered. "Then God will help you know what to do. God has promised this to all of us."

The people were sorry for their sins. They wanted to follow Jesus. They listened to Peter as he preached. More and more of them joined the group of Jesus' followers. And after Peter's sermon that first day, there were about three thousand new people who believed on Jesus!

Day after day, month after month, Peter and the apostles continued to preach and help people. With God's help, Peter healed a crippled beggar who then followed Peter and John to the Temple. When Peter began to preach to the crowd about Jesus, he and John were arrested. The leaders warned Peter and John about preaching in the name of Jesus. "You may go free this time, but there will be no more teaching in the name of Jesus," they said.

"We will have to obey God rather than the orders you give," Peter answered bravely.

So Peter continued to tell the good news of Jesus to people. Even when it wasn't easy, he still preached about Jesus.

Thinkback: Can you find some things in the pages you've just read which show that Peter was glad to have a second chance?

A Sword and a Prison

"Clang!" The iron gate of the prison slammed. Peter walked between two Roman soldiers. The heavy chains which bound him between the two soldiers clinked as they marched Peter to a cell.

"This Passover celebration is certainly noisy," one of the guards said.

"Yes," his companion agreed, "and the people were certainly pleased when Herod put the sword to that apostle James. That ended one of the troublemakers."

"Aye, and quite likely this one will be delivered to them after Easter. Those are Herod's intentions I hear."

"No chances are being taken," another soldier said. "Besides being bound to us with chains, there are fourteen of us between here and the iron gate which is tightly locked."

Finally Peter was settled into the prison cell, chained between the two guards. Fourteen other soldiers stood watch. Peter thought of the long hours ahead. He had been in prison before, but not quite like this. The anger of Herod and the crowds was very real to him.

Peter remembered his promise to Jesus that he would die for Jesus if necessary. "Am I to die like James? Is this the time that I will be put to death for my faith in Jesus just as he said I would be?" Peter wondered. But his faith was strong, and he had courage. Soon he fell asleep. And while Peter slept, his friends prayed for him.

Hours passed. Peter stirred in his sleep. Then he was wide awake. Someone had touched him on his side. A bright light shone in his prison cell. Before him Peter saw an angel. "Get up, Peter," the angel said. And as he was raised to his feet, Peter felt his chains fall from his hands. "Dress quickly," the angel continued, "and come with me."

Peter obeyed, wondering what would happen when the guards knew that he was free. Quietly they passed the first group of guards, then the second group. "Now," thought Peter, "what of the locked gate!" But he need not have wondered, for God had taken care of that also. When they reached the gate, it was opened for them.

The angel stayed with Peter through one street. When the angel left him, Peter hurried to the house where his friends were praying. He knocked on the door and a young girl named Rhoda came to answer. Peter spoke and waited to be let in. Rhoda could not believe her ears! She was so happy and excited that she forgot to open the door. She ran to

where the followers of Jesus were. "It's Peter! He stands at the door!"

"That cannot be true," they answered. "You must be dreaming."

Peter heard the excitement within. He kept on knocking. Then the door was opened, and the people were very surprised. In stepped Peter. He began to tell his friends how the Lord had brought him out of prison. "And, friends, be sure to tell all our brothers what a great thing the Lord has done for me. I must move on to another place."

45

The first streaks of pink began to show in the eastern sky. Peter remembered such mornings when he had brought a fishing boat to shore. He remembered a morning like this when he had eaten breakfast with Jesus beside the sparkling sea.

"God is not done with me yet," he thought. "I know that I must face death for my faith, but for now God still has other things for me to do. He has shown me this by setting me free from the hands of the enemy." And Peter hurried on with the good news of Jesus.

Thinkback: Was Peter afraid when he was in prison? Can you find a clue that shows he probably was not afraid?

• What did Peter's friends do when he knocked at the door where they were praying?
• Why do you think Peter moved on to another place instead of staying where he was?

Reflections

Dear Reader:

This page is to help you reflect on the life of Simon Peter, the prince of the apostles. You have already done some "thinking back." Now you may reflect on some important things about Peter's life and your life.

- What important thing do you remember about forgiveness from reading this book?
- Have you ever needed to be forgiven? How did you feel?
- Did Jesus use Peter's life even though Peter did wrong things? Why do you think Jesus could use Peter's life even though he did wrong?
- How can Jesus use your life?
- Even though we sometimes fail to do the right things, does this mean Jesus cannot use us again? What part of this book helps you know that?

A Special Message About Following Jesus

Peter became a follower of Jesus and gave his life to serve Jesus. To become a follower of Jesus is the most important thing you can do. Perhaps you have already made this decision, or maybe you have been thinking about it. This would be a good thing to talk with a grown-up about — your parents, your teacher, or your pastor. They can give you guidance for this important decision.